This book is for
my family and friends, who provided
endless encouragement and love;

for my husband Frank,
my partner in life
and biggest supporter;

for Luca,
who gave us hope
when we needed it
the most.

Cover by Zoe Saunders

ISBN: 978-0-578-95555-1 (hardcover)

Library of Congress Control Number: 2021915618

Far Apart,
Together at Heart

A children's book about COVID-19
and what we did to keep one another safe

Words by Kelliann Delegro   Illustrations by Zoe Saunders

The clock struck midnight, a year fresh and new.
We celebrated the arrival of 2020 and our excitement grew.

But after a few weeks, we heard bad news from around the world.

People were getting a dangerous virus,
and soon our worries swirled.

COVID-19 spread quickly, and many places had to close.

We had to wear a mask over our mouth and our nose.

Our favorite restaurants were closed and museums too,
Parks, beaches, playgrounds, schools, and even the zoo.

Students had to attend classes from their rooms.

Parents worked on their computers and met on Zoom.

Health care workers took care of people who got sick.

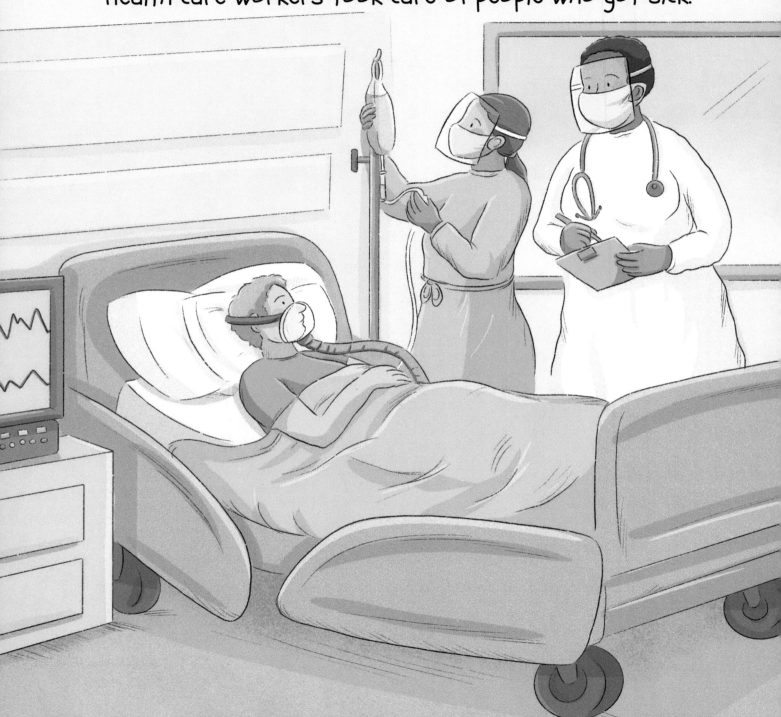

Others worked to deliver essentials we could order with a click.

We stayed home to stop the spread,

Spending time watching movies...

...and making bread.

We couldn't see or play with our friends.
Instead, many enjoyed finding new TikTok trends.

Grandparents, aunts, uncles, cousins, brothers, and sisters,
No one could gather for events or family pictures.

It was hard to stay far apart,
but we did what we knew was best.

We made crafts, danced, and baked
to keep from feeling stressed.

Technology was useful to help us stay in touch,
But despite our chats, we missed each other so much.

We only saw our loved ones on a screen
As we waited for scientists to create a vaccine.

Yet we learned that even though we were far apart...

Family and friends
remain together at heart.

Glossary

Coronavirus: a family of viruses (Coronaviridae) that causes many different types of diseases, including the common cold; a family of large single-stranded RNA viruses that have a lipid envelope studded with club-shaped spike proteins; infects birds and many mammals including humans.

COVID-19: a mild to severe respiratory illness that is caused by a coronavirus; 2019 refers to the year it was found. It is transmitted mostly by contact with infectious material (such as respiratory droplets and is characterized especially by fever, cough, and shortness of breath. SARS-CoV2 is the virus fully defined as "severe acute respiratory syndrome coronavirus 2" that causes the disease COVID-19.

Essential business: this definition varies between cities and states based on individual restrictions. Essential businesses are those that serve a critical purpose, such as grocery stores, pharmacies, waste collection, health care providers, gas stations, banks, transportation and agriculture services. Non-essential businesses served more recreational purposes.

Mask: a protective covering for the face or part of the face.

Pandemic: a worldwide outbreak of a disease; occurs over a wide geographic area (such as multiple countries or continents). Pandemics happen when a virus spreads easily and infects a large portion of the population.

Social distancing: the act of remaining physically apart in an effort to avoid direct contact with people in public spaces to minimize exposure and reduce the transmission of COVID-19. Social distancing can include working from home, the cancellation of events, and remaining at least six feet away from other individuals.

Vaccine: a substance that is administered (as by injection) to stimulate the body's immune response (produce antibodies) against a specific infection or disease.

Virus: Tiny organisms that can only be seen with special microscopes. These microorganisms are found all around us—in dirt, water, and in the air. Viruses can't survive for long outside of a living host (like a person, plant, or animal) because they need a host's energy to grow. Once inside a host, a virus can multiply and attack cells.

All definitions adapted from Merriam-Webster and National Geographic Kids.

About the Author

Photograph by Margo Millure Photography

Kelliann, born in Staten Island, New York, now resides in the suburbs of Richmond, Virginia. with her husband Frank and rescue dog Sebastian. Kelliann, with a bachelor's degree in English and journalism and a master's degree in publishing, has more than a decade of writing and editing experience. Her early career includes writing for her hometown newspaper, and she has spent most of her career working as an editor in the financial services industry.

Kelliann is the creator of @Bagels2Biscuits on Instagram, which showcases her love affair with food culture through area restaurants, family recipes, and her own culinary and confectionery creations.

"Far Apart, Together at Heart" is Kelliann's first book.

You can reach Kelliann by:

Email:
kelliann.delegro@gmail.com

Instagram:
@together_at_heart_book

Website:
https://kellianndelegro.wixsite. com/author

CPSIA information can be obtained
at www.ICGtesting.com
Printed in the USA
BVHW022002061121
620551BV00031B/752